Victorian Britain

TONY D. TRIGGS

This book is dedicated to Heather

ACKNOWLEDGEMENTS

The authors and publishers would like to thank the following for permission to reproduce photographs and other material:

Aerofilms Limited	5
Architectural Association	38; 39
Barnardo Photo Library	10
Beamish, The North Of England Open Air Museum	32; 42-43; 45; 47
By permission of the British Library	27
ET Archive	40
Hulton-Deutsch Collection	6; 8; 11; 19; 34-35; 46
Humberside County Libraries	13
The Illustrated London News Picture Library	35
The IronBridge Gorge Museum	21
Leicestershire Museums (Newton Collection)	15
Mansell Collection	5; 6; 8; 10; 12; 14; 22; 24; 29; 31; 36-37; 39; 44
Mary Evans Picture Library	7; 9; 12; 15; 16; 17; 18; 19; 20; 22; 23; 28; 37; 41; 45
Metropolitan Bradford Libraries	33
National Portrait Gallery	4; 29
Reproduced by permission of the National Postal Museum	13
By permission of the National Railway Museum, York	16; 17
Punch	26; 29
University Library, Keele	25
Wood Visual Communications	30-31
Yorkshire Mining Museum	21

The publishers have made every effort to contact copyright holders but this has not always been possible. If any have been overlooked we will be pleased to make any necessary arrangements.

First published 1992 by Folens Limited, Dunstable and Dublin.
Folens Limited, Albert House, Apex Business Centre, Boscombe Road, Dunstable LU5 4RL, England.

ISBN 1 85276109-1

Cover Design: Hybert Design & Type.

Printed in Singapore by Craft Print.

CONTENTS

Slums and widespread poverty in a land glittering with wealth.

1. The Victorian Age

From 1837 to 1901 Great Britain had a queen called Queen Victoria. In those days Britain was very powerful, and it ruled many overseas countries including Canada and parts of Africa. These countries made up the British Empire, and Victoria was their queen too.

British explorers like David Livingstone helped to make the Empire bigger. Livingstone explored the Zambezi river in southern Africa. Other British people then went to live along its shores, and they turned large parts of Africa into British colonies.

Britain was the world's greatest shipbuilding country; its navy helped to keep control of overseas countries and its cargo boats brought their cotton, rubber, metal and other products to Britain. British factories turned these products into finished goods. For example, the cotton was turned into cloth for making clothes. Then the goods were sold at a profit. Factory owners grew very rich but their workers were often badly paid, especially at the start of Victoria's reign.

There were many important changes during Victoria's reign. In 1837 most people lived in villages and worked on the land; by 1901 many had moved into towns to find work in factories, shops and offices. The growth of towns went on throughout Queen Victoria's reign, and so did the efforts to stop them getting too filthy and crowded.

A time of change

The two drawings below show Swindon (a town in Wiltshire) at the start and end of Victoria's reign.

1. Which drawing is the earlier one?
2. Why do you think so?
3. List some of the changes which you can see.
4. What things are the same?
5. What do the changes tell you about people's lives during Queen Victoria's reign?

In a time of change the Queen was a very important figure. She stood for things that mattered to people; for example, she made them feel proud to be British, and they admired her respectable family life. In 1887 and 1897 there were huge Jubilee (or anniversary) celebrations to mark her fiftieth and sixtieth years as Queen.

Is there a Jubilee Street near you?

Some towns have streets called Jubilee Street.

1. When do you think these streets were built?
2. See if your town has streets named after Queen Victoria, her husband Albert or the Jubilees. (A street map may help you.)
3. Try to check when the houses were built. (One of them may have a special stone which gives the date.)

Victorian children - rich and poor

Look at the photograph of the children below.

1. Which children are poor and which are well off?
2. How can you tell whether the girl with the basket is poor or well off?
3. Look at the well off children's faces. What might they be thinking?

This book is about life in Britain during Victoria's reign. This period (1837-1901) is sometimes called the Victorian Age.

The children grew up in the fresh country air; now they breathe smoke from factory chimneys.

A weaver's cottage

2. The Spread of Steam Power

For hundreds of years, villagers in Britain had farmed the land with sickles and other simple tools. As well as growing food for themselves they made their own cloth by spinning and weaving the wool from their sheep or the fibres from plants. Some earned money by spinning and weaving for businessmen who lived nearby. They did this at home, using simple tools which they worked by hand.

The power of steam

Look at the picture on page 7 which shows men working on a farm. The men have a steam engine. It runs on coal and can pull heavy loads along like a tractor. (This sort of engine is sometimes called a traction engine.) This time the engine is standing still and working the other machine, which threshes corn (beats it to separate the seeds from the stalks).

1. There is something in the picture that looks like a huge rubber band. What do you think it was for?
2. What do you think the sacks are for?

A home in the town

Life after steam

Pretend that you are one of the men working on the farm or a weaver working in a cottage, like the one shown on page 6.

1. Discuss with a partner how the coming of steam has changed your life.
2. Write a brief letter to a friend to describe the changes.
3. Compare your letters in groups - perhaps you could make up playlets in which people discuss the changes and argue about them.

When it is heated, water turns into vapour (or steam). The water vapour takes up a lot more space than the water. We can see this if we watch a saucepan of boiling water on a hob. The vapour needs a lot of room so it rushes out of the saucepan and rattles the lid. In a steam engine the power is carefully used to work machinery.

A large cloud of vapour turns back into a little water, and this change can also be used to work machinery.

The power of steam was not discovered until the end of the 17th century. The first steam engines were used to pump water out of flooded mines. Then, in the 18th century, they were sometimes used in factories to work machines.

Steam-powered machines could do spinning and weaving far quicker than they could be done by hand. Soon there was no paid work for people to do in their cottages, and countryfolk had to leave their homes and find jobs in the factories. By the start of Queen Victoria's reign enormous factories were being built, and towns for the workers grew up near them.

More people left the countryside as steam-powered machines replaced workers on farms. Thousands of families crowded into the towns each year and gave up all their old tools and ways of working.

‘Please, Sir, I want some more.’
‘What!’ said the master at length, in a faint voice.
‘Please, Sir,’ replied Oliver, ‘I want some more.’

3. Prison and Workhouse

Sometimes there were not enough jobs for everyone, even in towns with factories. Workers were often paid very badly, but those without work got nothing at all. Some families starved but others went to live in a workhouse.

A workhouse was like a prison; people were kept alive but were treated as harshly as possible. This saved money, since families avoided going there unless they were really desperate.

Husbands, wives and children had to live apart, and no one could have any outings, visitors, tobacco or beer.

Everyone - apart from old folk and disabled people - had to do back-breaking work. For example, they had to smash rocks to pieces, ready for use in mending roads.

The drawing above shows a workhouse yard and this one shows the separate stalls where men had to work. Why do you think they were kept apart?

In 1865 the *Daily Telegraph* described how a man had died at home because he could not face life in a workhouse:

He and his son used to work night and day repairing boots to try... and pay for the room... so as to keep the home together. On Friday night, when they had not even a halfpenny to buy a candle, he got up from his bench and began to shiver. He threw down the boots, saying, "Someone else must finish these when I am gone, for I can do no more." There was no fire, and he said,"I would be better if I was warm."

His wife... took two pairs of... boots to sell at the shop, but she could only get [enough for] coal and a little tea and bread, and her husband died on Saturday morning. When she was asked why they did not go into the workhouse the wife replied:
"We wanted the comforts of our little home."

Someone asked what the comforts were, for he only saw a little straw in the corner of the room, the windows of which were broken. The wife began to cry, and said that they had a quilt and other little things. Once, when the man applied... for aid, the... officer gave him a 4lb loaf and told him that if he came again he should get the 'stones'.

The son explained why they could not spend the winter in the workhouse:
"When we came out in the summer we should be like people dropped from the sky. No one would know us, and we would not have even a room. I could work now if I had food, for my sight would get better."

Home sweet home?

Read the description from the *Daily Telegraph.*

1. What do you know about the family's food, heating, lighting and bedding?
2. What happened to the boots once the family had mended them?
3. What do you think the officer meant by the 'stones'? (Look at page 11.)
4. What were the family's reasons for avoiding the workhouse?
5. After appearing in the newspaper the report appeared in a book by a writer called John Ruskin. Ruskin had it printed in red.
   Why do you think he chose this colour?

Life in the workhouse

Pretend you are in charge of a workhouse.

1. Write out a list of rules for people to obey. Include rules you have read about but also make up some rules of your own.
2. Perhaps you could turn your list of rules into a notice for the classroom wall.

Oliver Twist

The conversation at the top of page 8 comes from the novel *Oliver Twist* by Charles Dickens.

1. Where do you think it is taking place?
2. What is happening?
3. Why does Oliver have to ask twice?
   (Say what you think and then find out from the novel if necessary. The conversation takes place near the start of the novel.)

Thomas Barnado.
He provided hostels where hundreds of homeless children could live.

Some Victorians tried to help people who were being ill-treated. At the start of Queen Victoria's reign Elizabeth Fry called for better conditions in prisons, especially for women.

Better conditions

Look at the picture below which shows Elizabeth Fry visiting a prison.

1. Try to pick out Elizabeth Fry in the painting. What do you think she is doing?
2. Fry has brought some visitors to the prison. Which are the visitors and which are the prisoners? How can you tell?
3. What happened to children if their mothers were sent to prison?
4. Does this prison seem as bad as the one Dickens describes? In what way does it seem different?
5. Fry always tried to see every part of the prisons she visited.
   Why do you think this was so important?

Breaking stones.
What do you think the stones were used for?

Writers like Dickens made sure no one forgot the cruel way many workers and prisoners were treated.

For example, in *Pickwick Papers* he described a prison where people went if they were in debt:

Mr Tom Roker ... led the way through an iron gate.
"Oh," said Mr Pickwick, looking down a dark and filthy staircase, which appeared to lead to a row of damp and gloomy stone caverns beneath the ground ... "You don't really mean to say that human beings live down in those wretched dungeons."
"Live down there! Yes, and die down there, too, very often," replied Mr Roker; "and what of that?"

The evidence

Think about the report in the *Daily Telegraph* and what Dickens says in the *Pickwick Papers.*

1. Which do you think gives more reliable information? Why do you think so?
2. What do you think Mr Pickwick might have replied when Mr Roker said, "and what of that?"?
3. Try to make up some more of the conversation and perhaps write it out like a play or turn the story of the boot repairers into a play.
   (Hints: the man can go to the workhouse for help on the day he dies; that night his wife and son can talk to a friend about their very hard lives.)

Hang up my old whip over the fireplace; I shan't want it never no more.

4. The Railways

Until Queen Victoria's time most people spent their lives in the village where they were born. They might go to market in a neighbouring town but they rarely went further.

Some business people did make long journeys. Often they travelled in the horse-drawn stage coaches that linked London with other parts of the country.

Shorter journeys were usually made on foot or on horseback. Horses were very important indeed for transporting goods. They pulled farm wagons along country roads and they hauled heavy barges along canals.

They also hauled wagons of coal, stone and other supplies. Often the wagons were linked together to form long trains, and the horse pulled them along special tracks. Sometimes goods were taken from barges and put into wagons to finish their journey.

The horse-drawn 'trains' developed into proper railways. Steam engines fixed at the top of a hill were sometimes used to haul wagons up by means of chains. Then people started to fix an engine at the front of a train. The engine travelled along a track and pulled the train with it.

Stage coaches and trains

Read this page carefully and look at the pictures.

1. Who do you think said the words at the start of the chapter?
2. Why do you think he said them?
3. The painting on the left was done in Queen Victoria's reign. What was the artist saying about the two forms of transport?
4. Look again at this section and then write out the following sentences, filling in the blanks:

   At first trains were drawn by _____ or fixed _____. Then the _____ and _____ Railway opened. Most of the trains had _____ to pull them along. Soon there were railways everywhere, and people did not use _____ so much.

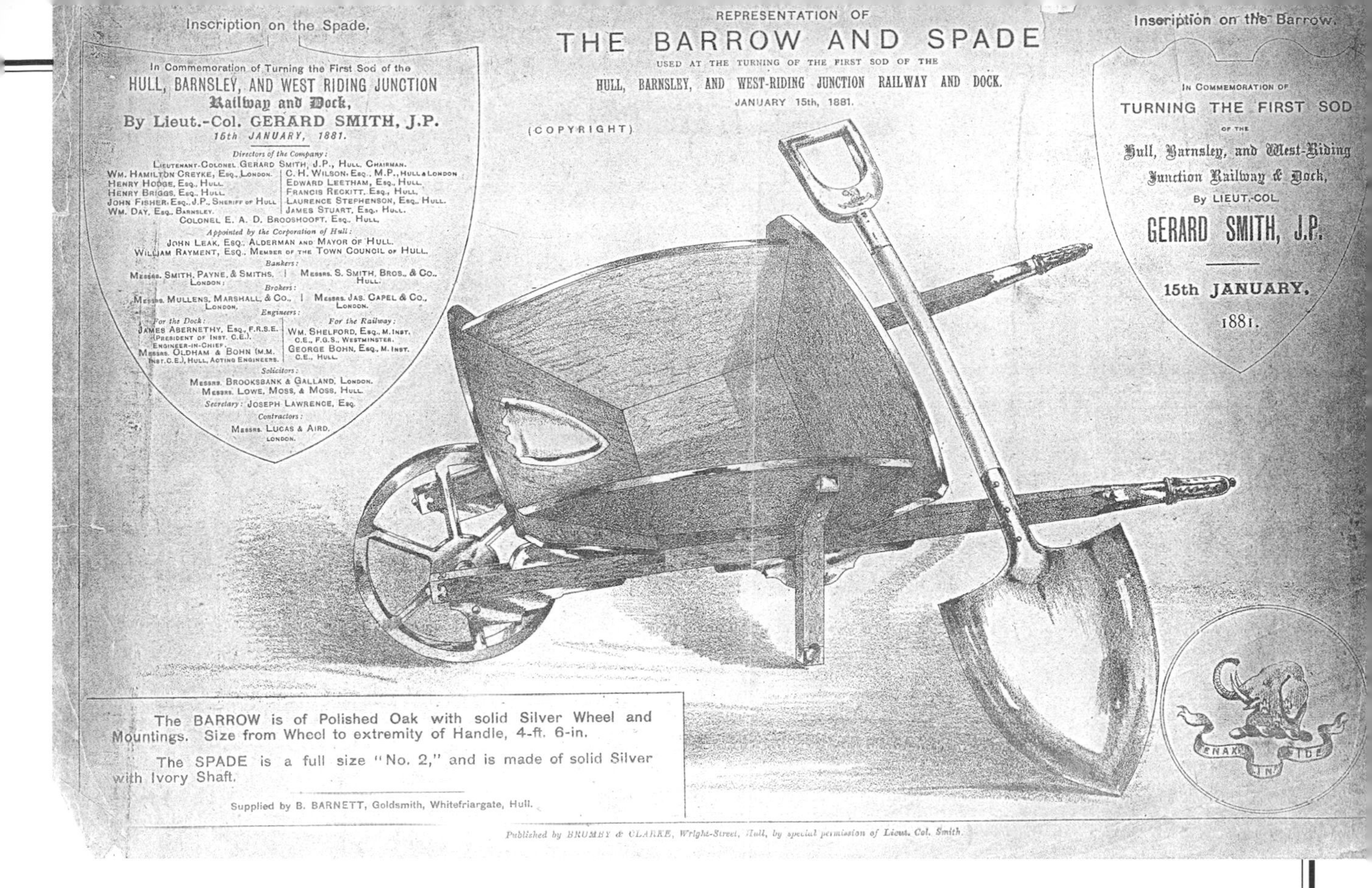

Discuss the event that is being advertised

A new railway

Pretend you live in Victoria's reign and a new railway is being built.

1. Design a poster for it.
2. If the railway was being built today, what changes would you have to make to your poster?

New railway tracks were quickly built. One of the most important linked Stockton and Darlington in the north of England. It was opened in 1825 and some people say it was the first proper railway in the world. Not only did the trains have locomotives (engines on wheels) but anyone could use them for goods or travel (other railways were private).

Railways were soon being built throughout Britain. By the middle of Queen Victoria's reign nearly every big town and village had a station.

A special year

Look at the picture of the stamp on this page.

1. The stamp appeared in 1975, 150 years after something special had happened. What was it?
2. Why was the event special?

There comes a crowd of burly navvies, with pickaxes and barrows, and ... the hills are cut through.

5.

NAVVY IN HEAVY MARCHING ORDER.

Navvies at Work

Railway builders had a very hard and dangerous life. The men (called navvies) worked with spades and barrows to take away unwanted soil. Often, the men lived in camps beside new railway lines.

A writer described the conditions at the time:

Some slept in huts constructed of damp turf, cut from the wet grass, too low to stand upright in ... Others formed a room of stones ... The rain beat through the roof, and ... the wind swept through the holes. If they caught a fever they died, or wandered in the open air, spreading the disease wherever they went. In these huts they lived with their women.

In 1846 a railway boss described to some members of Parliament how he treated his workers.

The men live in wooden buildings, with a room for cooking and ... hammocks slung along each side.

One man's wife cooks for the whole of them?

Yes.

You do not allow any other women in the camp?

No.

The navvy

Look at this page carefully.

1. List the things the navvy is carrying. In each case suggest why he needed it.
2. Look at the two descriptions of the navvies' camps. Which camp seems to be better? Why?
3. Who is asking the questions in the second paragraph?
4. Do you think the navvies would have liked a chance to give their opinions too? Why?

Some railway workers had come from Ireland to escape from starvation. Many Irish people lived on potatoes, which they grew on their own small plots of land. In the late 1840s the potato plants were hit by disease and the crops were poor.

Some Irish people found jobs and homes in English cities. Others helped to build railways. Because they were used to a very hard life they often did the hardest, most dangerous jobs, like digging tunnels and using explosives.

A hard and dangerous life

Think about the life of a navvy.

1. Suggest some of the dangers they faced in their work.
2. Make a poster to warn them of one or two of the dangers. (Few of them could read, so you will have to find good ways of illustrating your poster.)

A navvies' camp.
Which of the two descriptions opposite fits it better?

Rail Travel is a delightful improvement of human life. Man is become a bird; he can fly quicker than a ... goose.

6. The Effect of the Railways

A

Trains were much quicker than coaches. A train could travel from Scotland to London in one day or night; people going by coach had to sleep in different inns on the way. Shorter journeys might take half an hour by train instead of half a day by coach.

Travel became much cheaper and easier; a coach had room for ten or twelve people, a train could take hundreds.

People had different views about the trains. One man had this to say:

Everything is near, everything is immediate - time, distance and delay are removed.

Some people did not like the railways. This is what someone else had to say:

I detest railways. Your railway has cut through and spoiled some of the loveliest bits of scenery in the country.

Now, every fool in Buxton can be in Bakewell in half an hour, and every fool in Bakewell can be at Buxton.

B

C

Rail travel

Read page 16 including the introduction.

1. What effect did the train have on the journey time between Scotland and London?
2. What do you think is meant by 'Man is become a bird'?
3. Look again at what the people said about railways. What did they like and dislike about them?
4. Say what you feel about the points they made.
5. How do you and your friends think trains affected the following:
   - factory owners;
   - stage coach and canal companies and their employees;
   - towns like Swindon (look again at the pictures on pages 4 and 5);
   - seaside towns like Brighton;
   - the range of fresh food which people ate;
   - the spread of news and ideas;
   - the very poor.

First class travel?

Look at the three pictures at the top of these pages.

1. Describe the differences between the carriages.
2. At the start of Queen Victoria's reign someone wrote 'Get as far from the engine as possible'. Try to think of some reasons for this.
3. Which of the carriages do you think was nearest the engine?
4. Which of the carriages do you think was furthest from it?
   Say why you think so.

The poorest workers were forced to stay in their smoky cities, but others could live in smaller towns and travel to work; they could also go away for holidays.

Scotland to London

According to a Victorian writer, 'The early Scotsman scratches himself in the morning mists of the north, and has his porridge in London before the setting sun'.

1. Discuss what the writer meant.
2. Draw a poster to advertise the Victorian railways.

In Liverpool there were 7,860 cellars ... which were dark, damp and dirty. They were home for 39,000 people.

7. The Homes of the Poor

More and more Victorians could afford to travel, but some were so poor that they had to stay in their homes and factories.

Many mill workers' homes were cramped and filthy. The rows of houses were built 'back to back', and this meant that each house had other houses attached on three sides. Only the front of each house could have windows, and these looked out on a narrow road or alley-way.

There was usually one room upstairs and one room downstairs. A family of up to ten or twelve people might have to share this tiny home, and sometimes three or four of them had to share one bed.

Workers' homes

Look at the drawing below. Each little box represents a house. There is one detached house (a house with no houses joined on at all). The rest of the houses are joined in pairs or blocks.

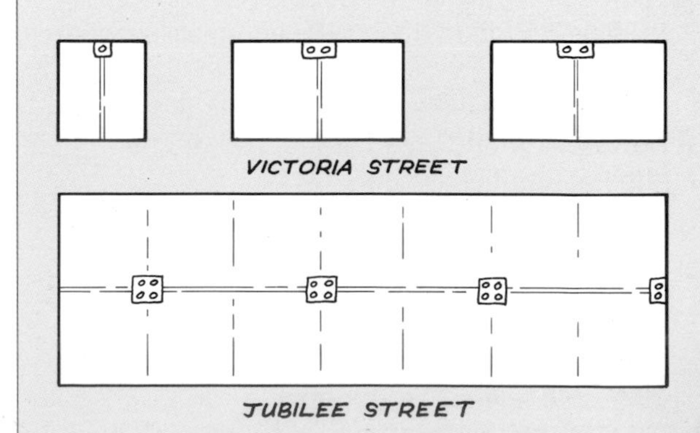

Some families had to live in cellars. A Victorian writer called Mrs Gaskell described a visit to such a home:

You went down into the cellar in which a family of human beings lived. It was very dark inside ... the smell was so fetid [foul] as almost to knock the two men down ... You could just see three or four little children rolling on the wet brick floor, through which the moisture of the street oozed up; the fireplace was empty and black; the wife sat on her husband's lair [bed] and cried in the dark loneliness.

Life in a cellar

The drawing below, done in Victorian times, shows a cellar home. Like Mrs Gaskell, the artist is trying to tell us about the lives of the poor. Use the drawing and Mrs Gaskell's description to help you answer the following questions:

1. How many people live in each cellar?
2. What is the worst thing about the cellar described by Mrs Gaskell?
   What do you think has caused this problem?
3. Why do you think the fireplace is empty?
4. A lair is a place where an animal hides.
   Why do you think Mrs Gaskell chose that particular word?
5. Look at the people in the drawing and study their faces. What do you think their feelings are?
6. What are the woman and oldest child doing?
7. Do you think the woman has warm or cold water? If it is warm how did she heat it?
   Where do you think she got the water?
8. Make a list of the problems and dangers facing families who had to live in cellars.

1. Find some back-to-back houses on the drawing.
2. Which houses have only one outside wall?
3. How many windows do you think these houses usually had?
4. How many windows do you think a cellar home had?
5. How many windows does your house have?
6. Do you think it is good to have plenty of windows? Why do you think so?

Factories and railways needed machines and engines which were made of metal. To get metal, Victorian workers heated special stone (called ore) until the metal inside it melted. Then they let the metal run into moulds to harden.

The stone was heated in giant ovens called furnaces. According to one Victorian writer:

The heat of the furnaces is terrible and the work most exhausting. The men have to wring their clothes when they get home...

"The work affects you all over," said a worker... "You get so cold that you shiver so you can't hold your food. The furnaces burn the insides out of you."

The man had burns all over his body.

If you didn't work you didn't eat.

8. Victorian Workers

A working life

Read carefully the descriptions of Victorian workers on these pages.

1. Why do you think the metal workers had to wring their clothes out when they got home?
2. One particular furnace worker is mentioned. What is wrong with him?
3. What word is used for a coal miner?
4. How can you tell that the cavern where the miner is working is small?
5. Describe what the children in the drawing on this page are doing.

Working in coal mines was just as unpleasant. Workers had to go down shafts (deep holes in the ground) to get to the coal. They climbed down ladders or were lowered on ropes, and there was always the chance of a terrible fall. At the bottom, the dangers were even worse. To get to the coal, they had to go along narrow tunnels. Sometimes there was so little room that they had to crawl on their hands and knees or slide on their stomachs. In the darkness they could hear water trickling down through the rocks. Perhaps the filthy puddles sometimes spilled into their mouths.

This is how a Victorian writer described the scene which a worker would find at the end of his tunnel:

In a cavern full of floating coal dust ... glimmer 3 or 4 candles stuck in clay. One hewer, nearly naked, lying upon his back, has his small, sharp pick-axe a little above his nose and picking into the coal ...

A life of danger

Using candles in a mine was especially dangerous.

1. Try to find out the reasons for this.
2. What other dangers faced Victorian miners? You can probably think of three or four by yourself (or with your friends).

Ancient or modern?

Look at the small photograph below. It was taken in a modern museum and shows what conditions were like for children who worked in the mines.

1. How well do the conditions match those shown in the drawing on page 20?
2. Do you think the museum used modern books or Victorian books for its information?
3. Which would be better? Why do you think so?
4. What other sources of information might the museum have used?

Iron works, Coalbrookdale

The streets are every morning wet by the tears of children who are forced by the fear of the strap ... to hasten, half dressed, to the worsted mills.

9. Work for Women and Children

At the start of Queen Victoria's reign women and children had to work for long hours, even if their jobs were very tiring indeed. In mines, the women and children had to take the coal to the wagons at the surface. The drawings (found in Victorian books) show ways of getting it through the tunnels and up the shafts.

This is what starting work was like for a seven-year-old called Robert Blincoe:

They reached the mill at about half past five ... Blincoe smelt the fumes of the oil on the axles of 20,000 wheels and spindles.

The task first given to him was to pick up the loose cotton that fell onto the floor ... Nothing could be easier, although he was terrified by the whirling motion and noise of the machinery, and not a little affected by the dust ... Unused to the stench, he soon felt sick, and by constantly stooping, his back ached ... But he soon found that sitting down was strictly forbidden. His task-master said he must keep on his legs. He did so for six hours and a half, suffering greatly with hunger and thirst.

Blincoe had grown up by the start of Victoria's reign but children were still being treated in the same harsh way.

Victorian children

Look at the girls in the photograph.

1. What do their faces say about them and how they feel?

A working life

Bosses were often harsh and cruel but they allowed their workers to have a lunch break.

1. Why do you think they gave them a break?
2. Mining families often worked together. Do you think they were paid by the hour or by how much coal they produced in a day? Why do you think so?
3. Pretend that you are a child who works in a mine or mill and write a letter explaining what your life is like. (You would need your Sunday School teacher's help - explain the reason for this in your letter.)

Women and children

Read these pages and look carefully at the pictures.

1. How did women and children move coal? How was this dangerous?
2. List some of the things which made Robert Blincoe's morning unpleasant.
3. Why do you think some workers only saw daylight on Sundays?

Working in mills could be almost as hard as working in mines. It was dangerous too, for workers sometimes got caught in machines, and growing children were crippled by all the bending and standing they had to do.

People believed that Sunday was a day for resting and attending church, so nearly everyone had this day off work each week.

Many churches ran Sunday schools, and this was the only schooling many children got. However, some were so tired that they fell asleep and fell off their benches during the lessons.

He cried when he had to climb the dark flues ...; and when the soot got in his eyes ...; and when his master beat him ...; and when he had not enough to eat.

10. Young Chimney Sweeps

For most of Queen Victoria's reign, chimney sweeps employed young children to go up chimneys and sweep them clean. The work was very dangerous, for the soot got into children's lungs and into cuts on their arms and legs.

An adult chimney sweep explained what life was like for a young chimney sweep.

The flesh must be hardened. This is done by rubbing it, chiefly on the elbows and knees, with the strongest brine. You must stand over them with a cane or coax them by a promise of a halfpenny if they will stand a few more rubs. At first they will come back from their work with their arms and knees streaming with blood and the knees looking as if the caps had been pulled off. Then they must be rubbed with brine again and perhaps go off to another chimney.

The best age for teaching boys is about six. But I have known at least two of my neighbours' children begin at the age of five.

Seven or eight years ago a boy was smothered (suffocated) in a chimney here. The doctor who opened his body said that they had pulled his heart and liver all over the place in dragging him down.

A law had been passed in 1840 to put a stop to the use of children, but people who broke the law were only fined a small sum, and most sweeps carried on as before.

Societies were formed to make sure that people obeyed the law. Some of these Societies offered to sweep people's chimneys without using boys, and they produced cards and leaflets to let people know about their work. The card opposite was produced in part of Staffordshire called the Pottery or Potteries.

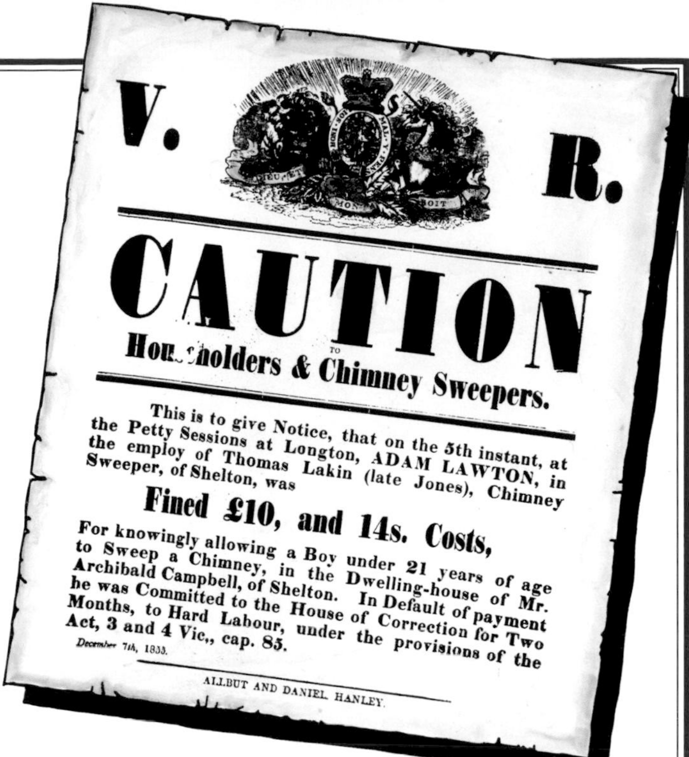

V. R.

CAUTION

TO

Householders & Chimney Sweepers.

This is to give Notice, that on the 5th instant, at the Petty Sessions at Longton, ADAM LAWTON, in the employ of Thomas Lakin (late Jones), Chimney Sweeper, of Shelton, was

Fined £10, and 14s. Costs,

For knowingly allowing a Boy under 21 years of age to Sweep a Chimney, in the Dwelling-house of Mr. Archibald Campbell, of Shelton. In Default of payment he was Committed to the House of Correction for Two Months, to Hard Labour, under the provisions of the Act, 3 and 4 Vic., cap. 85.

December 7th, 1855.

ALLBUT AND DANIEL, HANLEY.

Now and then

Think about life today.

1. Why do you think there was more need for chimney sweeps in Victorian times than there is today?

Chimney sweeps

You will need to read these pages carefully.

1. Find out what brine is. What did chimney sweeps use it for?
2. How can you tell that the brine must have hurt?
3. What were the dangers children faced when they went up chimneys?
4. What could sweeps use instead of children?
5. Look at the poster and briefly explain what it says. Who do you think produced this poster? Why do you think they produced it?
6. It was against the law for anyone to let a boy go up a chimney. As well as sweeps, who else could be fined? (If you need a clue look again at the poster.)
7. Why do you think people risked a fine rather than changing their methods?

Climbing boys

Look at the boy in the picture and read the poster on this page.

1. Pretend that you are the boy and produce your own poster asking people to stop using 'climbing boys' (young child sweeps).
2. Pretend that you are the sweep who was fined and make up a speech to tell the court why you think you have done nothing wrong. Perhaps you feel that you treat your climbing boy well.

The cripples might be numbered by hundreds, perhaps by thousands ... They seemed to me, such were their crooked shapes, like a mass of crooked alphabets (letters).

THE "SILENT HIGHWAY"-MAN.

11. Better Conditions for Workers

Some people cared very deeply about how workers were treated. One of these people was Lord Ashley, who later became the Earl of Shaftesbury.

Shaftesbury and others called for changes to stop children being worn out and crippled by their work. In 1833 (four years before the start of Queen Victoria's reign) Parliament passed a Factory Bill. It banned the use of children under nine in mills and it put a limit on older children's working hours. However, the hours were still very long, and adults were not protected at all. In any case, some employers simply ignored the new laws.

In 1842, Parliament banned the use of women, girls and young boys in coal mines. Then, in 1844 and 1847, it made further cuts in the number of hours that women and children could work in mills. Children from nine to thirteen could work for up to six and a half hours a day, and women and older children could work for up to ten hours a day. Mills could not keep going without women and children, so the working day for everyone (including men) quickly fell to about ten hours.

Parliament tried to see that younger children had some part time schooling, and schools were often set up at factories. Parliament appointed inspectors to check that the laws were being obeyed. It also passed new laws to help people in workshops. Nail-makers' workshops were cruel places where each nail had to be hammered into shape by hand, but at least there was now a limit on the workers' hours. Finally, in 1875, Parliament made a tough new law that stopped the use of climbing boys.

At the start of Queen Victoria's reign very few homes had their own water supply. Some homes did not even have a toilet, and the family had to pour their slops into the gutter. Other homes had a toilet just outside the door, but it did not flush and the filth went into a hole in the ground. Rain sometimes washed the filth from gutters and toilets into workers' homes. It even got into the water they used for drinking and washing, which came out of wells and public taps. Sometimes the water looked and smelled dirty; but even when it seemed to be clean it was full of germs, and deadly diseases like typhoid spread through many cities. In the centre of Manchester most people died before they were 20.

Early in Queen Victoria's reign a man called Edwin Chadwick said that every home should have its own toilet linked to a sewer (a large pipe under the ground to carry the waste away). He also said that every home should have clean running water. By 1901 (when Victoria died) flush toilets, sewers and running water had all been provided, and people had stopped building back-to-back houses. As a result, there was far less disease.

Health conditions

The map below appeared in 1842 in Chadwick's famous book *The Sanitary Condition of the Labouring Population of Great Britain.*

1. Try to find out what sanitary means.
2. Say what the map shows.
3. What sort of home would have been flooded most often?
4. The cartoon at the top of page 26 was drawn in Queen Victoria's reign. What do you think the artist was trying to say?

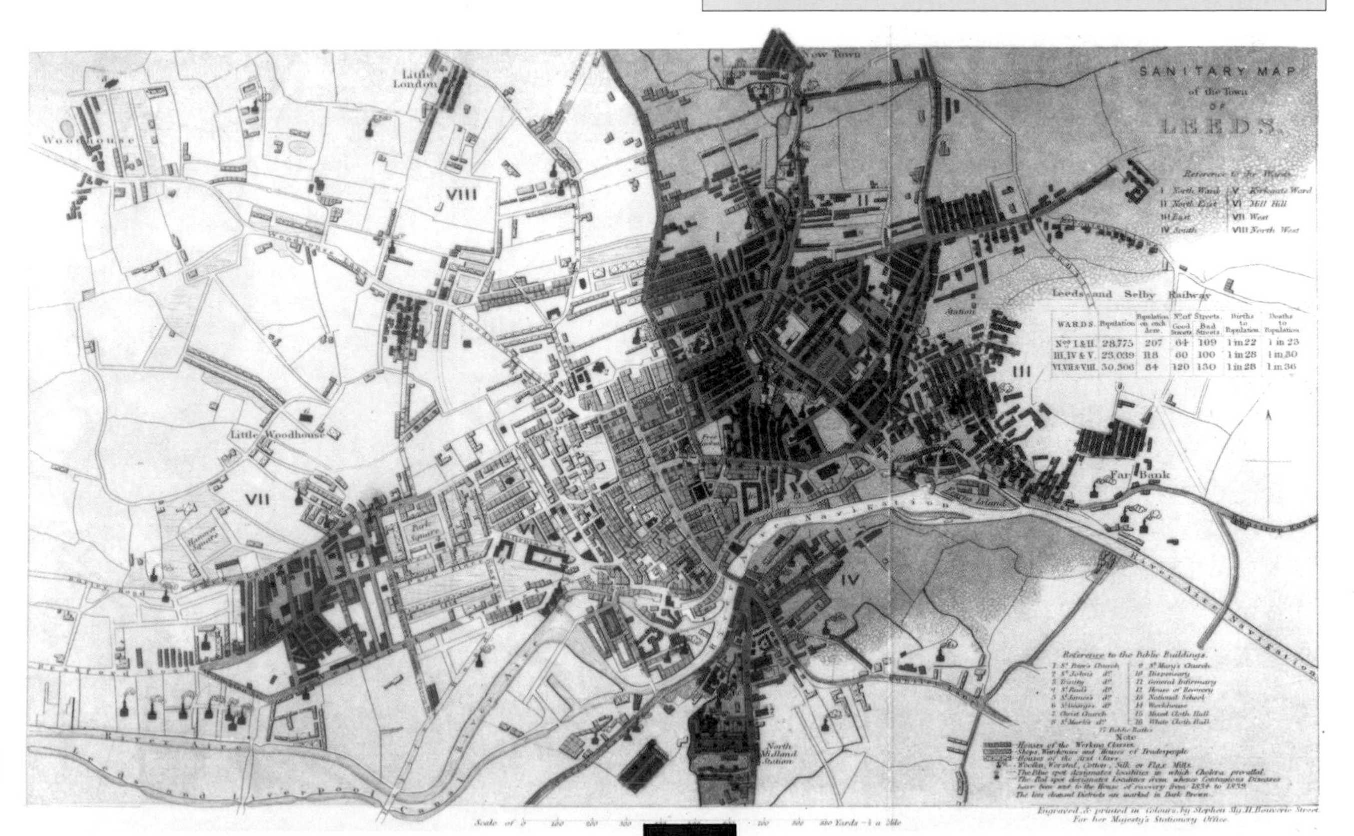

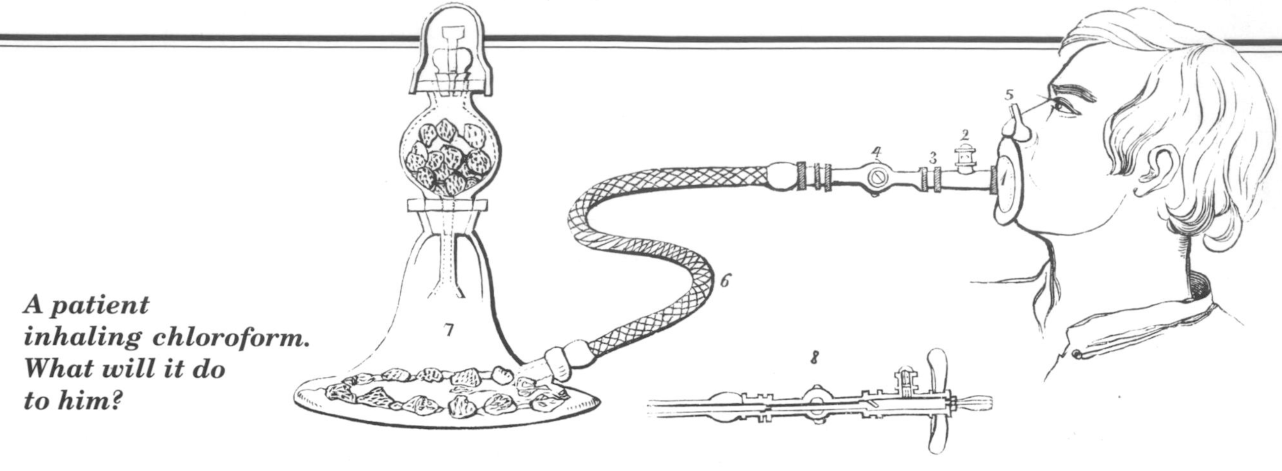

A patient inhaling chloroform. What will it do to him?

Medical treatment also improved. At the start of Queen Victoria's reign it was hard to carry out operations. Doctors had no reliable way of easing pain, and a team of men had to hold the screaming patient down. Surgeons had to be very quick, and could only do simple operations like cutting off legs. They could not do any delicate work inside patients' bodies. During the 1840s the problem was solved by the use of anaesthetics (drugs such as ether and chloroform, which deadened pain).

Surgeons using chloroform could do all sorts of new operations, but some patients died because germs got into their wounds.

Doctors were only beginning to understand about germs, but a Scottish surgeon called Joseph Lister began to use an antiseptic (or germ-killing) spray during operations. Later, he and other surgeons simply kept themselves, their tools and their hospitals as clean and germ-free as possible.

Thanks to Chadwick's ideas, Victorian people began to live long and healthy lives. And if they did fall ill they could often be treated and cured.

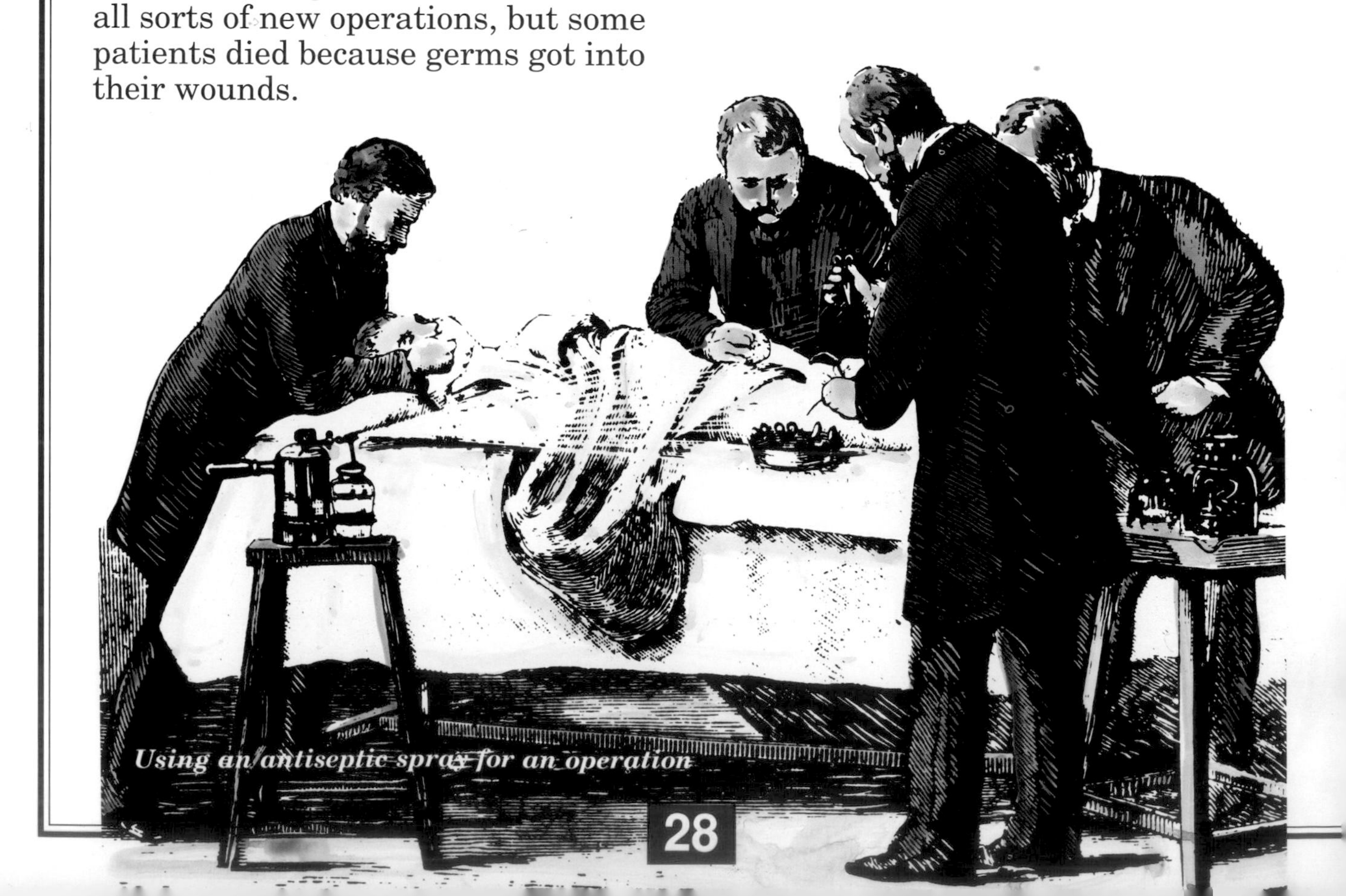
Using an antiseptic spray for an operation

An English nurse called Florence Nightingale went to the Crimea (southern Russia) to tend soldiers wounded in battle there. She helped to spread the idea that nurses and hospitals should be clean.

This drawing includes two pictures of Florence Nightingale's face. What was the artist trying to say about her?

Florence Nightingale, at Scutari

? Improvements in medicine

Some Victorians felt it was wrong to use anaesthetics, especially for easing the pain of childbirth. They pointed out a Bible verse that seemed to say that giving birth was meant to be painful. However, in 1857 Queen Victoria used chloroform herself.

1. What effect do you think her action had on other people?
2. What advice might Florence Nightingale have given to the nurse in the drawing on the right?

THE NURSE.

About 3,000 persons are employed in the works; and 756 houses have been built for them, each with a separate yard and toilet.

12. Saltaire Village

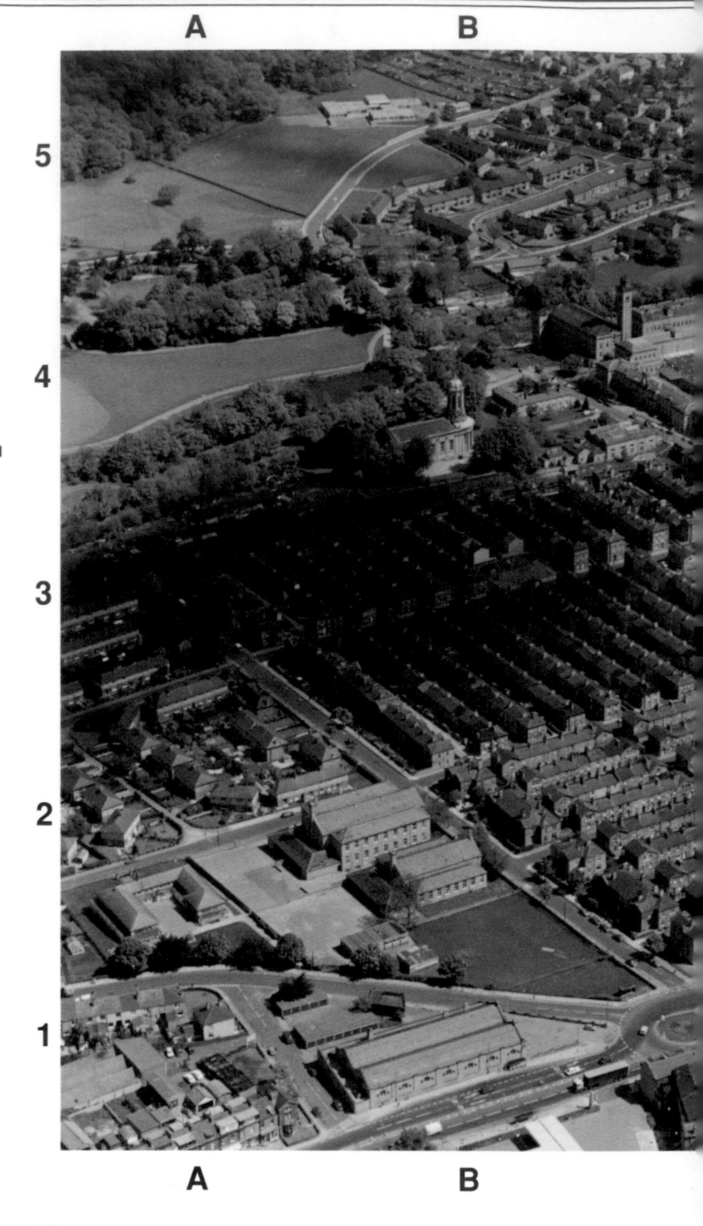

As we have seen, there were many mill owners who treated their workers cruelly, but others tried to meet their needs and give them homes that were fit to live in.

One man who treated his workers well was Sir Titus Salt. In the 1850s he built his own spinning and weaving mills, along with a village to house the workers.

Salt made sure that everything was clean and healthy. He chose a site in the Yorkshire countryside, well away from the smoke and filth of the nearest cities (Leeds and Bradford). Because the village was totally new it needed a name, and Salt decided to call it Saltaire (made up from his own name and that of the nearby River Aire).

There were no oozing gutters outside the doors, for every house had a toilet linked to underground drains. There was water on tap, and every home had gas lamps, at least in the downstairs rooms. There were lots of large windows to let in plenty of daylight and air, and some houses even had their own gardens. No wonder workers were glad to rent the houses for only 1s (5p) a week!

Most of the houses in Salt's village had two rooms downstairs and two rooms upstairs. The rooms were small but at least there was no need for parents and children to share a bed.

Saltaire from the air

The village included a church, a park and a library for the workers to use.

Saltaire

Look at the photograph of Saltaire from the air. It will help you to answer the following quesitons.

1. Was the photograph taken in Salt's time or ours? How do you know?
2. Do you think all the houses shown in the photograph were built by Salt?
3. Try to pick out some of the housing built in Salt's time. Use the grid to help you.
4. Can you find Salt's mill?

Now look at the photograph at the bottom of the page. It shows Saltaire shortly after it was built.

5. Suggest some of the ways in which goods and people travelled to and from the village.
6. The village had no public house. Why do you think this was?
7. At the end of some blocks of houses there were larger houses. Suggest which workers might have lived there.
8. One house had a tower where someone could keep an eye on the villagers. How do you think they felt about being watched in this way?

A village for the workers

Pretend that you are a worker who has just moved from the centre of Leeds to Saltaire.

1. Write a letter to someone who still lives in Leeds and tell them about the things that are different in Saltaire. (They may not believe you, so you can ask them to come on the train to see for themselves. The journey takes 20 minutes and they may be able to save up the fare.)

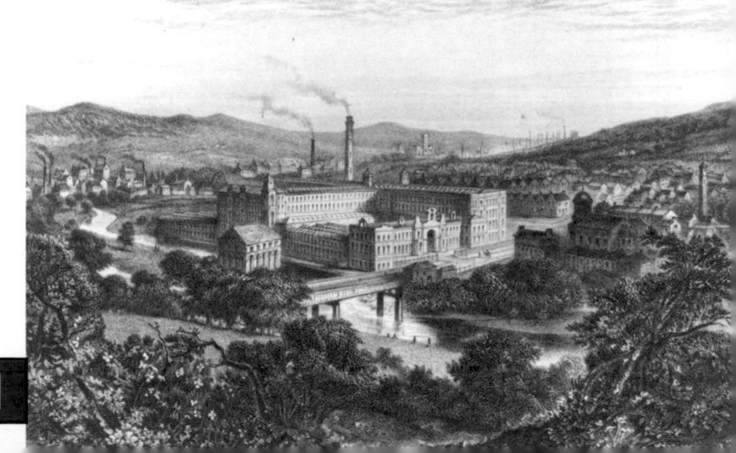

The rich man in his
castle,
The poor man at his
gate,
God made them, high or
lowly,
And ordered their estate.

13. Masters and Servants

Hymns like 'All Things Bright and Beautiful' encouraged the poor to accept their hard lives while rich folk lived in luxury. Salt's workers had homes with only two rooms, but a nearby mansion called Milner Field had over 50 rooms. There was a billiard room, a library and a music room with a huge organ. There was also a giant conservatory with marble statues and tropical plants. Every room was as comfortable and fine as possible, with beautiful carpets and chandeliers. The mansion was owned by Titus Salt (Sir Titus Salt's son).

Salt had a horse-drawn coach to take him wherever he wanted. To reach the mill he travelled down a tree-lined drive and across his own bridge. Salt and his family had over a dozen maids and servants. They treated them well but they had to work hard.

Many Victorian girls became maids, though few worked in mansions like Milner Field. Some worked in farm-houses; others found jobs in the homes of well-paid workers like bank managers. They had to sleep in the cellar or attic, and often they shared it with other maids and perhaps a number of mice or rats.

Maids were paid just a few pence a week but they got enough food to keep them alive. It was usually better to become a maid than to stay at home in a filthy slum.

Maids had to do all sorts of housework, and in those days it was harder than it is today. For example, there were no washing machines, and maids scrubbed clothes on a scrubbing board or put them in a tub and beat them with a stick called a 'dolly'. Often, there was a housekeeper telling the maids what to do - and boxing their ears if they did it wrong.

Victorian washday

Look at the photograph on page 32.

1. Try to find out what each of these items was called.
2. Why do you think the 'dollies' have slots at the bottom?
3. Look again at pages 30 and 31 and think about Salt's life and his home. Then list some of the things his maids and servants might have had to do.

Milner Field mansion

What was the artist trying to say in this drawing?

Rich and poor

Look again at pages 30 and 31 and then pretend that you and a friend are workers at Sir Titus Salt's mill. Perhaps one of you thinks he is kind and good but the other thinks he is greedy and selfish.

1. What might you say to each other about the things he has done for himself and his workers? You could each write two or three sentences.
2. Pretend that you have just left school at the age of ten and are writing home after one week's work as a maid. Tell your parents about the way the work is affecting your hands.
3. Discuss why the verse at the start of this chapter is usually missed out when people sing the hymn today.

I never went to school.
I got no clothes to go in.
I cannot read or write.
I don't know what you
mean by God.

14. Schools

At the start of Queen Victoria's reign few children went to school, and they grew up unable to read or write. Church registers (records) of marriages show that only half of the people who married could sign their names.

The government did not run any schools. Some people ran small schools in their homes. Larger schools, called charity schools, were built and run by wealthy people who wanted children to learn about God and Jesus Christ.

Most charity schools had a single class and just one teacher, who taught the pupils how to read the Bible and Prayer Book. She also taught them writing, arithmetic, and perhaps some skills like sewing and gardening.

Charity schools for the very poor were called 'ragged schools'. One man explained:

When we first opened the school no less than five boys came absolutely naked except for their mothers' shawls which were pinned around them. Five separate gangs of thieves attended the school.

Schools often charged a few pence a week, and many parents could not afford it; others needed the money their children could earn at work. Because of this, most children left before they were ten. The man who founded the ragged school said that the thieves were 'all, within six months, earning their [livings] more or less respectably'. For some children, work and school went together. Children in textile (cloth) mills often worked in the morning and studied in the afternoon. Some bosses even provided a school-room at the mill.

Do the children in this classroom all look fit and well?

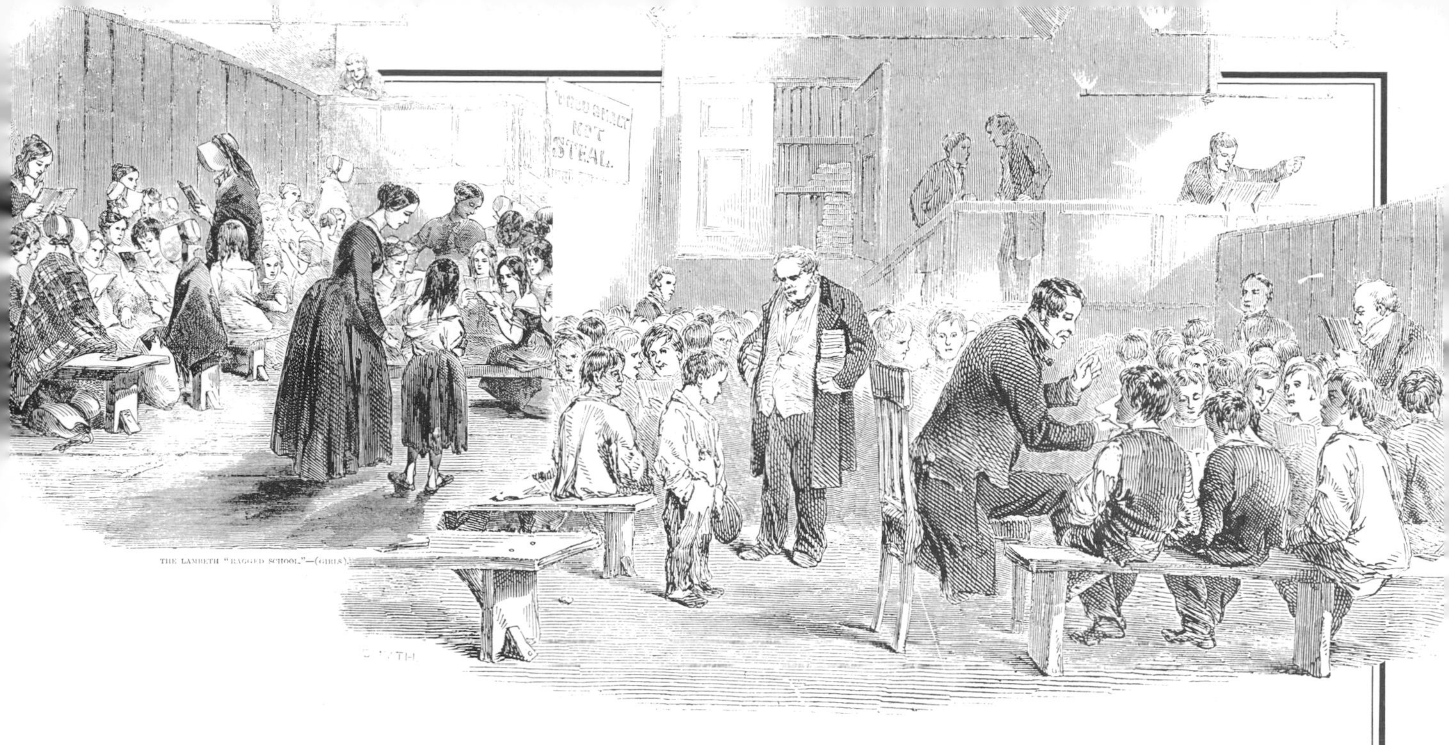

In 1843, Charles Dickens said the following about a ragged school at Field Lane in London.

It was held in a low-roofed den in a sickening atmosphere in the midst of ... dirt and disease ... The pupils ... sang, fought, danced, robbed each other - seemed possessed by legions of devils.

A few years later he said it was:

Quiet and orderly ... well white-washed, numerously attended, and thoroughly well established.

What do you think might be wrong with some of them?

Other schools were run by churches. As well as providing Sunday schools they began to open more and more day schools. Often, there was a teacher and over a hundred pupils in one large room. It was hard to keep order; bad behaviour was punished severely, and many children were caned until they bled. Older pupils, called monitors, did a lot of the teaching. They stayed behind after school for extra lessons. Then, next day, they taught small groups of younger pupils.

Some schools were very poor indeed. A government inspector said that at one school:

The children were playing in the open yard, and the master was... sawing up the blackboard. His books and materials for teaching... consisted of six Bibles, some copy books, one slate, half a dozen loose and ragged leaves of Reading Made Easy and the remains of the blackboard ... supported on either side by a hand-saw and a hammer.

Queen Victoria's government wanted every child to go to school, and they also wanted to make schools better and less overcrowded. In 1870 they told local councils to set up their own schools if extra places were needed. Then, in 1876, a new law said that children must go to school until they were 12 or 13.

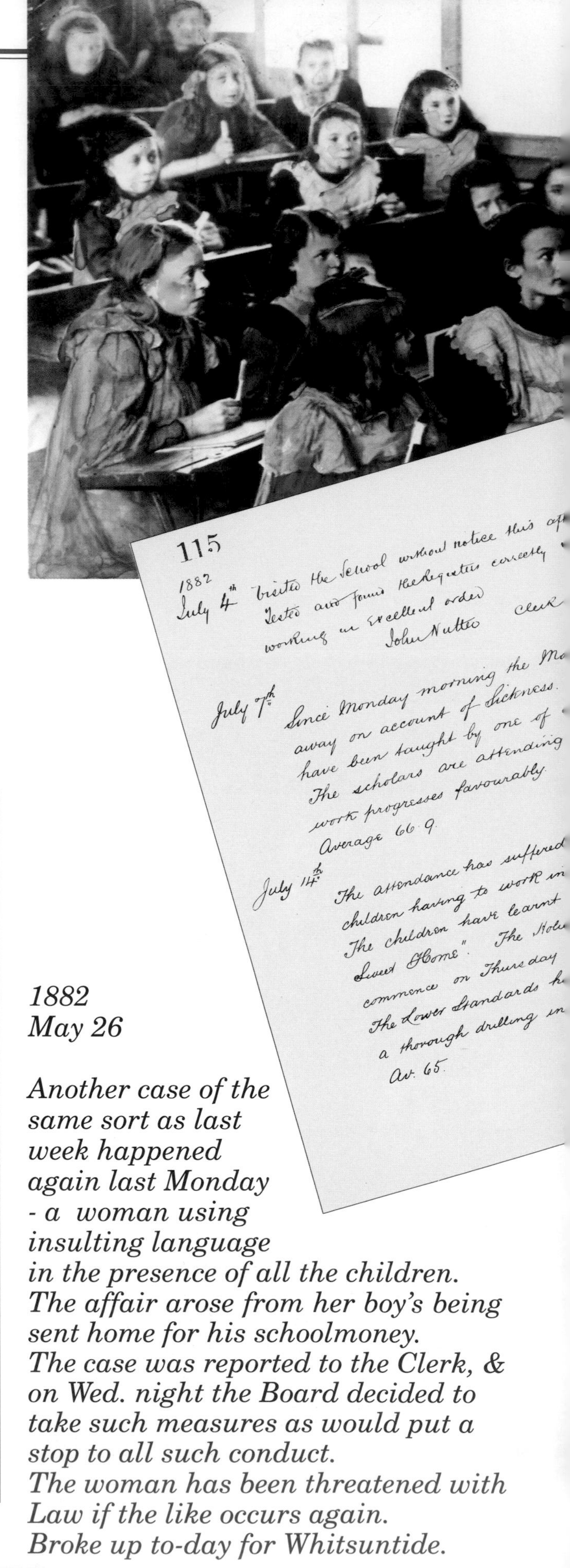

115

1882 July 4th Visited the School without notice this aft
Tested and found the Registers correctly
working in excellent order
John Nutter Clerk

July 7th Since Monday morning the M
away on account of Sickness.
have been taught by one of
The scholars are attending
work progresses favourably.
Average 66.9.

July 14th The attendance has suffered
children having to work in
The children have learnt
Sweet Home". The Holi
commence on Thursday
The Lower Standards h
a thorough drilling in
Av. 65.

Ragged schools

Think about what you have read about schools.

1. How do you think 'ragged schools' got their name? Do you think children had to pay to attend them? Why?
2. The man who founded the ragged school did not mention teaching the children to read or teaching them about the Bible. What did he seem to care about most?
3. Why do you think the teacher was sawing up his blackboard? Find out why teachers and pupils used slates in Victorian schools.
4. In 1842 a teenage boy said: "I cannot read much ... I have read the spelling book and Ready-ma-deasy. I cannot write." What do you think he meant by Ready-ma-deasy? (Read this page again if you need a clue.) What does his mistake tell us?
5. Look at the photographs. How were Victorian classrooms different from yours?

1882
May 26

Another case of the same sort as last week happened again last Monday - a woman using insulting language in the presence of all the children. The affair arose from her boy's being sent home for his schoolmoney. The case was reported to the Clerk, & on Wed. night the Board decided to take such measures as would put a stop to all such conduct. The woman has been threatened with Law if the like occurs again. Broke up to-day for Whitsuntide.

In Victorian times, the teacher at each school had to keep a 'log' (a sort of diary listing the main events). These extracts are from the log that was kept at Eldwick School, in Bingley, West Yorkshire. (One entry is given in modern printing as well as in the Victorian writing.)

113

May 26. Another case of the same sort as last week happened again last Monday — a woman using insulting language in the presence of all the children. The affair arose from her boy's being sent home for his schoolmoney.
The case was reported to the Clerk, & on Wed. night the Board decided to take such measures as would put a stop to all such conduct
The woman has been threatened with Law if the like occurs again
Broke up to-day for Whitsuntide.

June 9.
On Monday 3 new scholars were admitted. The week's work has been carried on very briskly, and the children have profited by it.
A friend, who is a Student in ~~a~~ the Glasgow Training College has been here 2 days. He has Standards I & II in hand, who, I think, require special drilling. The Routine will be departed from for a few weeks, Sewing taking place on Monday and Monday's work being done on Wed, so that the Assistant may have Tues. Wed & Thurs. here. Stands. I & II are having shorter Lessons & greater variety. Av. 63.2

Drawing is now taken as first Lesson in morning and afternoon to prepare for Exam. next monday.

Drawing Examination took place this morning. Messrs Fox and Naylor were present. 27 scholars were examined in Freehand.

List of Object Lessons from January 30 to Mch 20/83.

Date	Lesson	Master
Jan 30	The Camel	P.T.
Feb 2	The Reindeer	M.
" 9	The Orange	P.T.
" 13	The Ostrich	M
" 16	Paper	P.T.
" 20	The Whale	M
" 23	Sugar 3rd list	P.T
" 27	The Silkworm	M
Mar 2	The Beaver	P.T.
" 6	Rice 3rd List	M
" 9	Cocoa "	P.T.
" 13	Coffee	M.
" 16	Tea	~~P.T.~~
~~20~~	[illegible]	

School logs

Study the 3 pages from the school log.

1. What made the mother angry?
2. What do you think 'schoolmoney' was?
3. John Nutter belonged to the Board (or Committee) which ran the school. Why do you think he came 'without notice'?
4. Some teachers still choose monitors to help with jobs. Why would it cause more problems if a monitor was away in Victorian times?
5. Look at the third page from the school log. What do you think an 'Object Lesson' was? What do you think the initials mean? Whose initials do you think they are?
6. How does the children's schooling seem to differ from yours? (You can discuss this and then make a list of points.)
7. Pretend that you are a pupil at Eldwick School in the 1880s and write a 'log' or diary from your own point of view. You can write about some of the days in the real log. For example, what was it like for you when the angry mother arrived?

A blazing arch of lucid glass
Leaps like a fountain from the grass
To meet the sun.

15. Public Buildings

The Victorians were proud of their towns and cities, and they showed their pride by building magnificent town halls and libraries, many of which are still in use. They were also proud of their success in business, and we still use some of the market halls and corn and cloth exchanges they built.

Near to their towns the Victorians built sewage and water works so that people could have clean streets and clean water. At Papplewick near Nottingham the water works had steam-driven pumps to send the water to people's homes. The pumps can still be seen inside the very fine Victorian building. The Victorians showed how important they thought clean water was by decorating the inside with all sorts of water and wild life designs.

Papplewick Pumping Station nr. Mansfield

How are they different?

The photographs on these pages show Victorian buildings.

1. How are they different from modern buildings?

Crystal Palace, 1851

Companies sometimes wanted people to lend them money, perhaps to buy new stock or new ships. They knew that people would only do this if the company seemed to be doing well, so they showed their wealth by spending as much as they could on their buildings. Railway companies were especially keen to attract new investors, and some of their stations look like palaces!

Victorian buildings

Think about the buildings in a town near you.

1. Try to decide if any large buildings in this town look Victorian, then check their dates.
2. Make a list of some large Victorian buildings you know about, including ones you have seen in this book and ones in your town. If you like you can add a note to say what the building tells you about the Victorians. Your own ideas are best but here are two examples:
   Saltaire Church - workers were expected to go to church every Sunday;
   St Pancras Station - more and more railways were being built.

Public buildings

Look carefully at these pages.

1. What do you think was done in corn and cloth exchanges?
2. Nowadays we rarely think about water and sewage works. Why did the Victorians care about them so much?
3. Why were the Victorians able to build huge archways and domes? Where can we see huge archways which the Victorians built?

The Victorians built real palaces too. One of these is the Palace of Westminster, also called the Houses of Parliament. This has lots of towers and spikes, but the Victorians found out how to use metal to make archways and domes. Victorian stations have large arches, and the Albert Hall in London has an enormous dome.

It was not possible to cross the road without having to wade ankle deep in mud or water.

16. Streets and Shopping

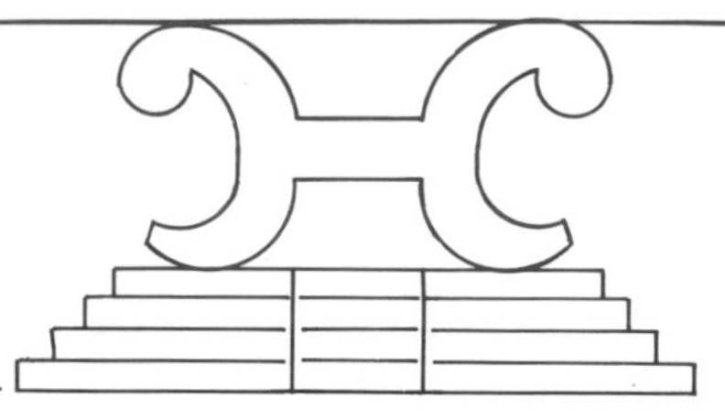

Some people had one of these just outside their door. What do you think it was for? Why did they need it?

Muddy streets made shopping hard, especially for women in their long skirts. The Victorians solved the problem of mud by making more and more of their roads from pebbles or blocks of stone. However, shopping could still be dirty and difficult. By the 1870s most new houses had proper toilets but there were more and more horses fouling the streets. Cart-wheels sent filth everywhere, and the noise they made was deafening.

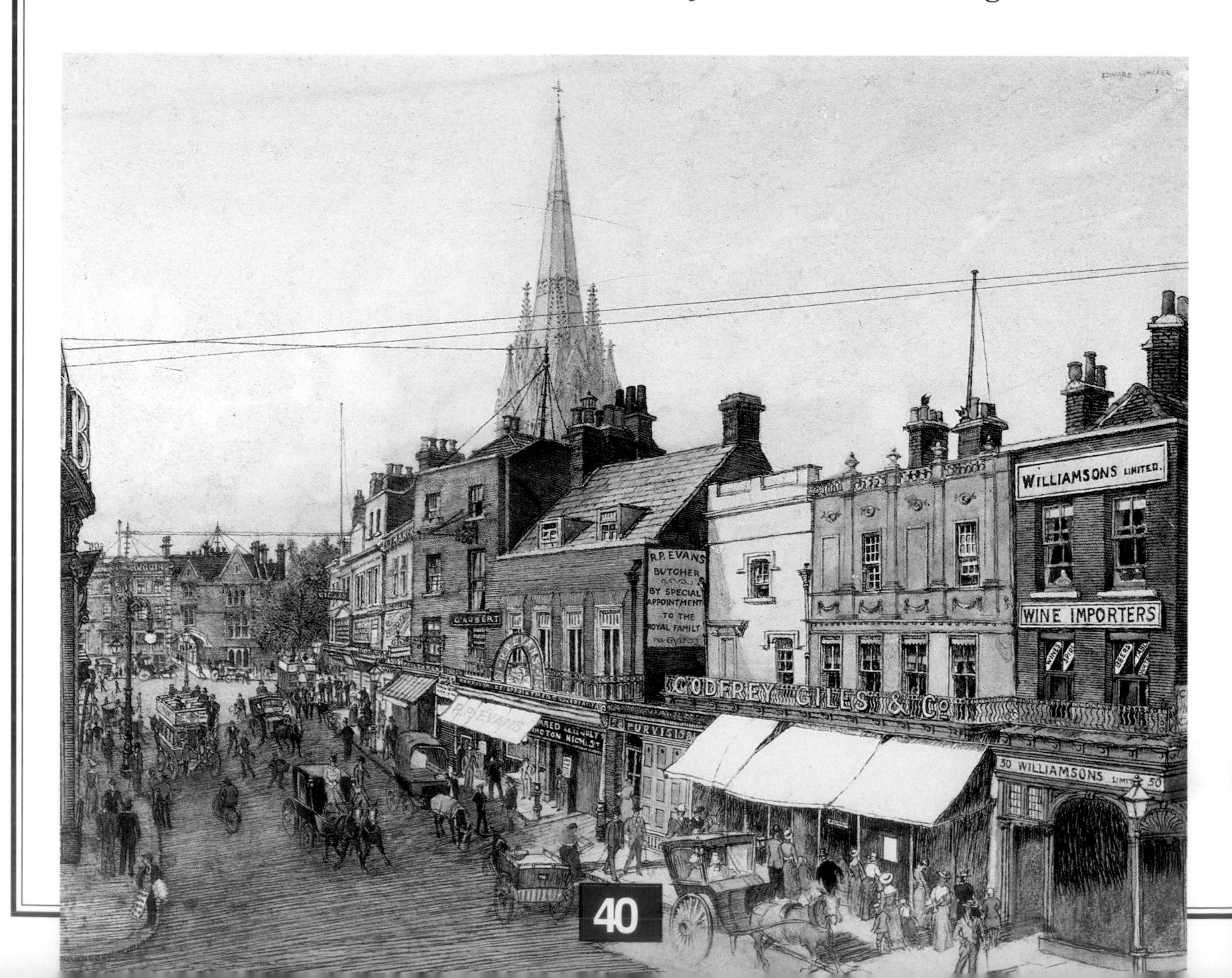

This is how Dickens described a morning scene in a London street:

Now and then a stage coach covered with mud rattled briskly by ... The public houses, with gas-lights burning inside, were already open ... Then came ... groups of labourers going to their work, then men and women with fish-baskets on their heads, donkey carts laden with vegetables, carts filled with livestock or ... meat, and milk-women with pails ... It was market morning. The ground was covered nearly ankle deep with filth ... , and a thick steam ... rising from ... the bodies of the cattle mixed with the fog, which seemed to rest upon the chimney tops ...

Victorian shops

The painting on this page was done in 1898, 28 years after Charles Dickens' death.

1. Why do you think it differs so much from Dickens' description? (Try to think of more than one reason.)
2. Why do you think Victorian shops had signs as well as their name in words?
3. What sorts of places still have signs today?
4. Look at the passage by Charles Dickens. Why are there cattle, horses and donkeys in the streets?
   Dickens mentions fog and chimneys. How do you think the two were connected?
   Some of the people are going to market but one lot are going from house to house. Which people do you think they are? (Hint: we still have the same thing delivered today.)

Wagons and saddles

The Victorians had shops where saddles and other leather goods were made and sold. They also had shops for repairing wagons.

1. Design your own simple signs for these shops.

Shops were usually small, gloomy rooms in the owner's home. The photograph shows a grocer's shop. Most of the goods were in tubs or sacks, and the grocer used his scales to weigh what each customer wanted. Butter and sugar were in huge blocks; the grocer cut and shaped each customer's piece of butter with two wooden 'patters'; he sold the sugar in lumps which the customer had to break up.

Chemists' shops had shelves full of strange-looking packets and bottles. Often, the chemist had mixed these medicines up himself, using plants and chemicals. He put Latin names on the labels to make the medicines seem special. He also put big pointed bottles of coloured water in his windows. They helped to show which shop it was and they made it look strange and mysterious.

Other shops also had signs. For example, a pawnbroker's shop had three golden balls above the door. People went there to borrow money, and the balls represented bags of gold.

Delivering the milk

Victorian milkmen and milkmaids took buckets from door-to-door and they poured the milk into people's jugs. Sometimes they had carts but sometimes they carried the buckets themselves. The buckets were too heavy to carry round the streets in their hands.

1. Find out how they carried the weight on their shoulders.

Victorian shopkeepers

Many shopkeepers had boys with bicycles who delivered people's shopping for them and collected their orders. Nowadays, 'grocers' boys' and 'butchers' boys' are almost unknown.

1. Why do you think this change has occurred? (You and your friends may be able to think of several reasons.)
2. Think of some shops near you where the owner lives and works and think of some shops where no one lives. Which are more like Victorian shops? Which do you prefer? What are the main differences?

The churches got us to their evening meetings by giving us food. One church gave us potatoes and another gave us buns. We used to dash from church to church grabbing all we could.

17. Food and Drink

What people ate depended on how well paid they were, and this was linked to the job they did.

In his famous Report, Chadwick gives us clues to the diet of different workers:

The weaver lives on very innutritious poor food, seldom eats meat;
Irishmen subsist chiefly on potatoes;
The collier [coal-miner] ... drinks too much ... and both he and his family partake of animal food every day.

The mill worker has tea, sugar, bread and butter night and morning; meat, and either bread or potatoes, with a pint of beer every day for his dinner.

Traders known as hucksters sold 'tea, coffee, sugar, butter, cheese, bacon... and other articles to the working people in small quantities'. They charged a very high price and said that this was to make up for people failing to pay their bills. Some traders cheated the poor by selling them food that was stale. For example, they smeared fresh blood over meat that was going bad.

The Victorians had some clever ways of studying what different groups of people ate. For example, they found out the weight of cattle that were driven to a market, then they found out how many people lived in the area. In Manchester, there was enough fresh meat for everyone to have a helping each day. However, the meat was not shared fairly: most of it went to the better-paid workers; the poorer ones had to make do with salted meat like bacon.

Even when parents had enough money they sometimes fed their children badly, since they did not know which foods were best. Doctors complained that children were being given 'bacon, fried meat and fatty potatoes when they had not, perhaps, two teeth in each jaw'. Parents also gave them drugs to send them to sleep; and some parents made themselves drunk in the evenings to forget their hard lives.

Diets improved as trains brought more and more fresh food into city centres. For example, Londoners started to eat Yorkshire rhubarb, and milk reached cities all over the country.

Victorian cooking

Look at the photograph above.

1. The woman in the picture is standing near a cooking range. Pick it out and say how the cooking was done. Where do you think bread was put to bake? Suggest what sort of fuel was used.
2. What do you think the bucket was for?
3. Do you think cooking would be easier and safer in this room or in a modern kitchen?
4. What noises and smells might you notice if you were in this room?
5. Name one or two objects in this room which we would not see in a modern kitchen. Name one or two things which look different from ours. How are they different?

Victorian kitchen

Look at the pictures on this page.

1. Do you like the look of this room?
2. Do you think the woman liked it?
   Discuss these questions with a partner.

Well off people had meat, but this did not always keep them healthy. A Victorian child wrote in her diary:

At dinner time Papa gave Emily a choice piece of pheasant [wild bird] with bread sauce and potato, but she refused the pheasant... so Papa took it to dear Leo ... It was the last thing he ate that he enjoyed.

Victorian diet

Find out what you can about the Victorians' diet.

1. Suggest what the woman in the photograph might have had for each of her meals on a single day.
2. Try to make a nice-looking menu for her main meal but keep the food simple!
3. Pretend you are old and that the woman in the photograph is your grandmother.
   Write a paragraph beginning with the words, "I can still remember visiting my grandmother one afternoon ..."

For most adult workers the public house or music hall had all one could wish for - warmth, bright lights, music, song, companionship ... Beer was the quickest way out of the city.

18. Pleasures and Pastimes

Children usually played in the streets, but for some who were free on a Saturday there was football on a local pitch.

Travelling shows were very popular. There were jugglers, fire-eaters and men with monkeys and dancing bears. There were also Punch and Judy shows in towns and on beaches.

People who went by train to the seaside often took a dip in the water. Men sometimes swam completely naked, but women changed in bathing machines. A bathing machine was a hut on wheels, and the woman could be wheeled right into the water to bathe in private.

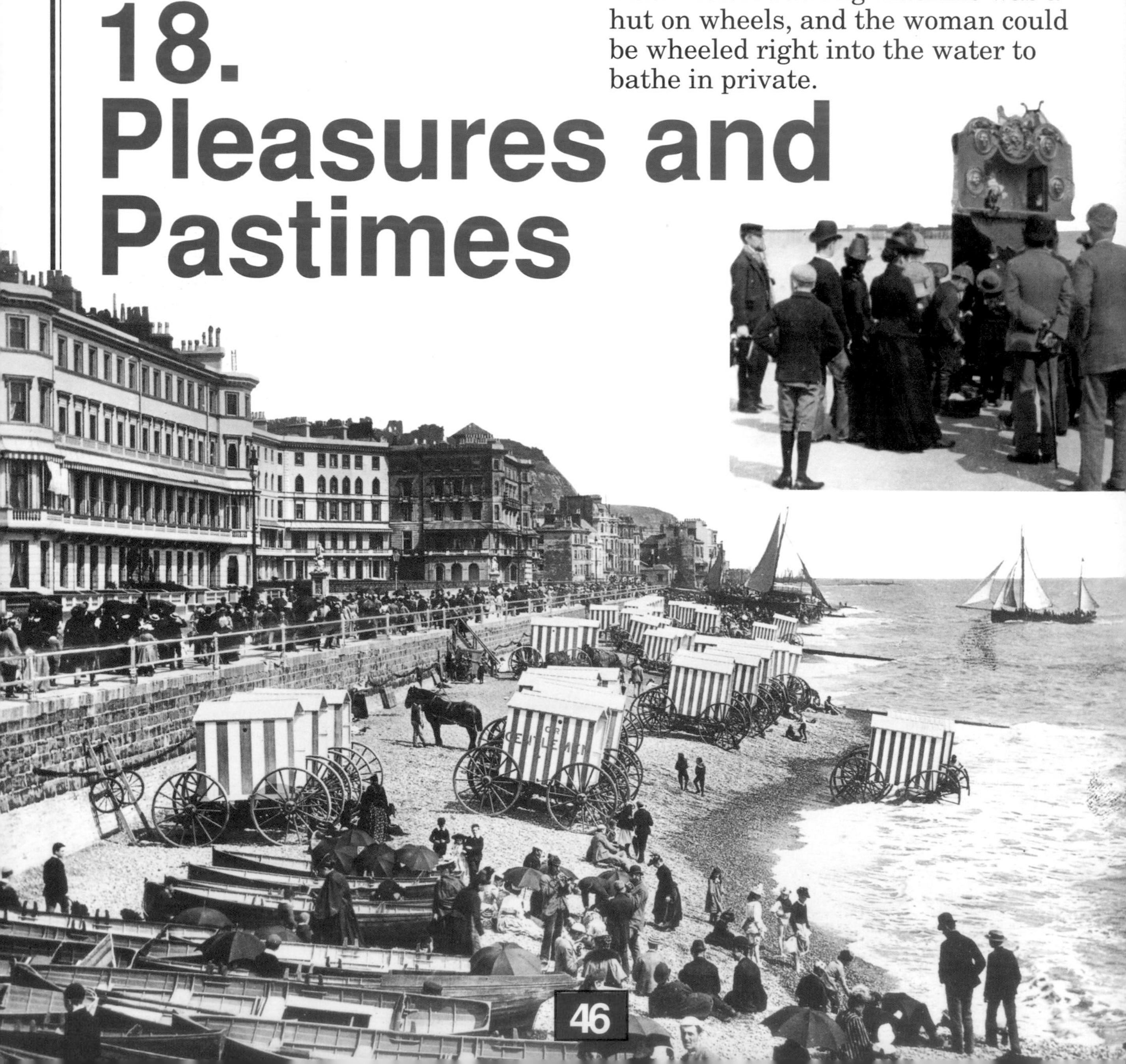

Parents drank to forget their hard lives, and children played with simple toys like marbles, skipping ropes or tops.

Balls were too expensive to buy but sometimes they could make their own. One child explained:

In November came pig-killing time. Soon our ears would be tormented with the screams of the expiring [dying] pig; ... we hung round waiting for the bladder, which ... we blew up with a clay pipe stem.

Victorian games

Read these pages and look carefully at the pictures.

1. Use your own words to explain how some children made balls. Do you think you would find this sort of ball in the house in the photograph? Why?
2. List all the toys you can recognise in the photograph. How do they differ from toys today?
3. What did children of your age do on Saturdays? What did they do on Sundays?

Pleasures and activities

Look through these pages again.

1. Make a list of all the toys and activities, putting one on each line.
2. Now put a tick by any which we still have today, a cross by any we do not have, or a comment to say how things have changed. Perhaps your list will begin like this:

Toy or activity	Comment
Playing football	Victorian children sometimes made their own balls
Watching shows in the street	

3. How well off were the girls who went to the toy fair compared with other Victorian children? Why do you think so?

Town councils provided parks, libraries, museums and zoos. They wanted workers to use their spare time in a healthy way, learning new things and taking exercise. Employers and councils disliked drunken, noisy behaviour and Saltaire did not have a single pub! On summer evenings the workers could sometimes row on the river; for a treat they could go to a nearby fairground, where some of the rides were driven by steam. Better-off families had nurseries with all sorts of toys, and the children could sometimes buy themselves new ones:

To spend an afternoon at the winter Fair ... was like a visit to fairyland, because ... they entered from the gloomy street into a brightly gaslit interior... A brass band played lively marches, and the air was filled with a strong smell of wax dolls ... The smallest room... contained toys ... for a penny. Whatever money came the girls' way during the year had to be saved for a spree in this room.

Index